Is This a
TIGER?

To Sofia Isabelle Parton and Yaroslav Polivar — E.E.

Published in Canada and the U.S. by Kids Can Press Ltd.
25 Dockside Drive, Toronto, ON M5A 0B5

Kids Can Press is a Corus Entertainment Inc. company

www.kidscanpress.com

The artwork in this book was rendered digitally.
The text is set in Pleuf Pro.

Edited by Patricia Ocampo
Designed by Marie Bartholomew

Printed and bound in Buji, Shenzhen, China, in 3/2024 by WKT Company

CM 24 0 9 8 7 6 5 4 3 2 1

MIX
Paper | Supporting responsible forestry
FSC® C010256

Library and Archives Canada Cataloguing in Publication

Title: Is this a tiger? / Elina Ellis.
Names: Ellis, Elina, author, illustrator.
Description: Series statement: Alex's field guides ; 2 | Includes bibliographical references.
Identifiers: Canadiana (print) 20230560792 | Canadiana (ebook) 20240294556 | ISBN 9781525306754 (hardcover) | ISBN 9781525308789 (EPUB)
Subjects: LCSH: Tiger — Juvenile literature. | LCSH: Endangered species — Juvenile literature. | LCGFT: Picture books.
Classification: LCC QL737.C23 E45 2024 | DDC j599.756 — dc23

Kids Can Press gratefully acknowledges that the land on which our office is located is the traditional territory of many nations, including the Mississaugas of the Credit, the Anishnabeg, the Chippewa, the Haudenosaunee and the Wendat peoples, and is now home to many diverse First Nations, Inuit and Métis peoples.

Alex's Field Guides

Is This a TIGER?

Elina Ellis

Kids Can Press

Hello, my name is Alex,
and this is Atticus.
He has never seen a TIGER!

I will show Atticus a real tiger.
I know everything about tigers.
I have even made a journal about them.

Tigers are the LARGEST wild cats in the WORLD.

Superstrong jaws and teeth

Tigers have fake eyes on the back of their ears called OCELLI.

Circular pupils

White tigers have blue eyes.

They are used to confuse predators and prey.

Some teeth are 8 cm (3 in.) long.

At night tigers can see **6** times better than humans.

Over **100** stripes. No two tigers have the same pattern.

5 whisker types all over their bodies to sense, navigate and gather information

The stripes are on their skin, too.

Very strong and muscular legs

Can leap 9-10 m (10-11 yd.) and sprint 50-65 km/h (31-40 m.p.h.)

Weigh up to 300 kg (662 lb.)

That's like **10** ten-year-olds

The tiger is the national animal of **INDIA.**

70% of all wild tigers live in India.

Tigers make all sorts of SOUNDS.

A tiger's roar can be heard up to 3 km (1.8 mi.) away.

Grunt

Growl

Roar

Hiss

Snort

Chuff

Meow

Snarl

Tigers can't **PURR** like most cats.

TIGERS LOVE

Swimming

Playing

Zzz
Sleeping

Exploring

Grooming

TIGERS LIVE IN

Siberian taiga

Swamps

Grasslands

Rain forests

There are **NO** wild tigers living in **AFRICA.**

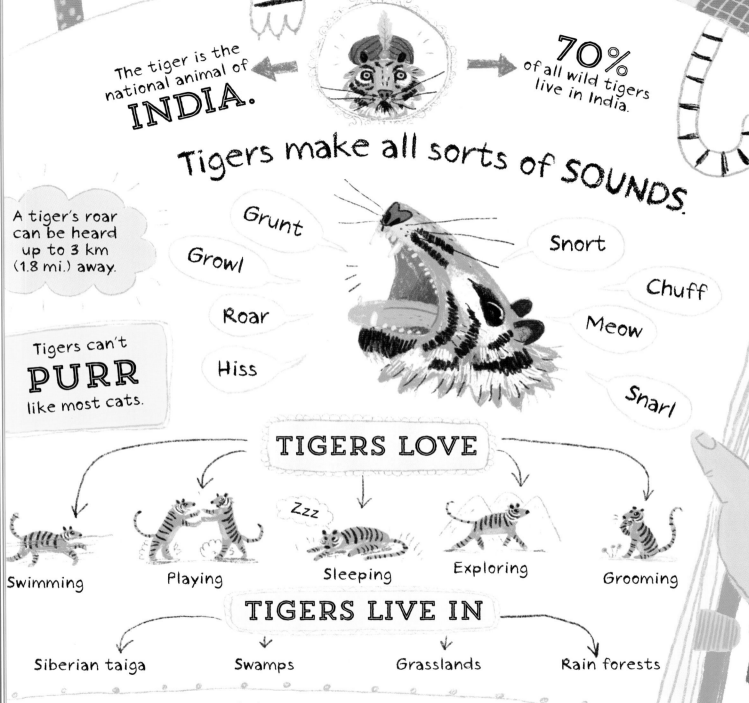

That's a lot
of teeth! This is
SURELY
a tiger.

No.

No.

No.

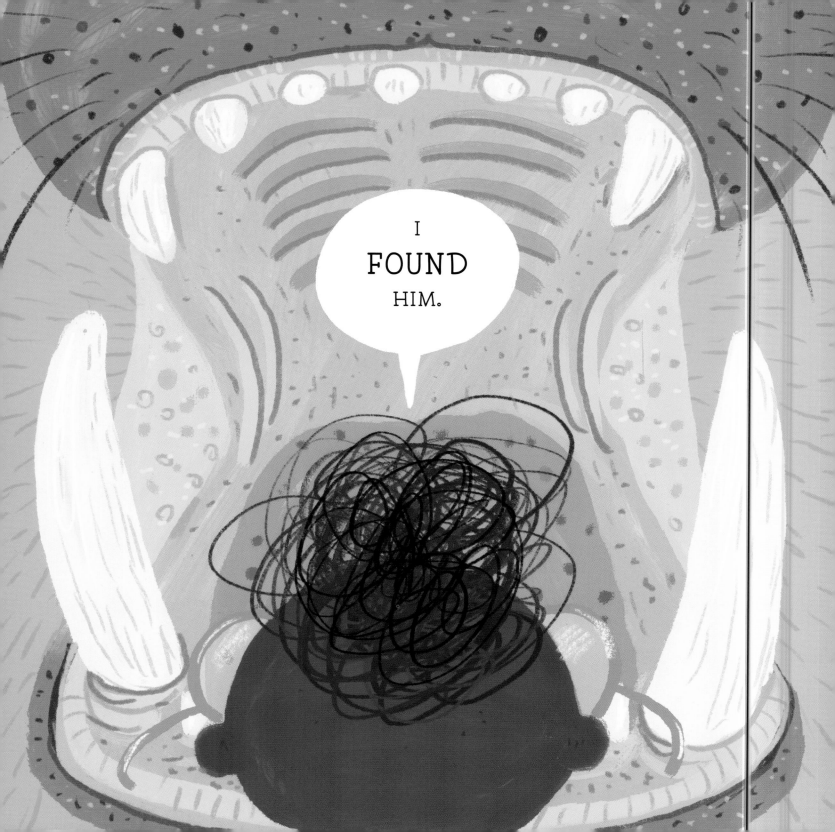

Tigers hunt at NIGHT (they are also carnivorous...).

They still have a very diverse diet.

Deer

Bears

Wild boar

Buffalo

Rodents

Crocodiles

Rhinos

Antelope

Birds

Fish

They even eat insects!

TIGERS EAT

Tigers can eat up to **40** kg (**88** lb.) of meat in a single go.

Tigers are solitary hunters. They search for food alone at night.

When they hunt, tigers rely on their eyes, ears and whiskers and not that much on their nose.

Tigers are stalk-and-ambush hunters. They hide in wait and then pounce on their prey unexpectedly.

Tigers don't eat at the kill site. They drag their prey into cover.

Tigers don't like to share! Each tiger can roam up to **100** km (**62** mi.) in search of their own food, water and shelter.

A tiger eats about **50** deer-sized animals each year (about **1** per week).

Tigers are ENDANGERED
(which means not many of them are left in the world).

Out of the **9** types of tigers known, only **6** are still around.

Siberian tiger

- Biggest tiger and has pale, thick fur
- Can take down a bear
- 450-500 left in the wild

Bengal tiger

- Oldest, most well-known species
- White belly and bright orange fur
- Around 3000 left in the wild

Indochinese tiger

- Incredible night vision
- Golden fur and white belly
- 250-300 left in the wild

Malayan tiger

- Similar to Indochinese tiger
- Long whiskers and piercing yellow eyes
- Fewer than 200 left in the wild

South China tiger

- Small tiger with reddish fur
- Very long stripes
- 30-40 left in the world

Sumatran tiger

- Smallest species
- Very dark stripes
- 300-400 left in the wild

Caspian tiger

EXTINCT

Bali tiger

EXTINCT

Javan tiger

EXTINCT

Tigers are really old animals. They were around **2 million years ago!**

BUT

Over the last 150 years, the tiger population has shrunk by nearly **95%**.

DANGER

WHY ARE TIGERS DISAPPEARING?

Poachers hunt them for their pelts, meat and body parts.

Humans have taken **35%** of tigers' forests for crops, timber, roads and cities.

Necklace

Potion

HOW CAN WE HELP?

Spread the message

Did you know?

Donate $ to "adopt" a tiger

Learn more

Dear President ...

Write to governments and newspapers

TAKE CARE OF THE ENVIRONMENT

Reduce

Reuse

Recycle

Creatures Atticus met in this book

CAT

Shares 95.6% of its genes with TIGERS

NUMBAT

Has a long, sticky tongue to eat ants

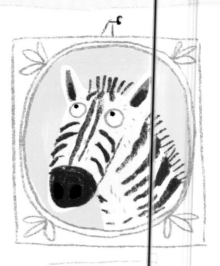

ZEBRA

Can sleep standing up

LEMUR

Lives only in Madagascar

WARTHOG

Doesn't actually have any warts

WALRUS

Can run as fast as a human

...that are definitely not TIGERS!

SHARK

Doesn't have a single
bone in its body

HIPPO

Loves water but
can't swim

BAT

Can eat up to 1000
mosquitoes an hour

SKUNK

Is immune to snake venom

OWL

Can turn its head
270 degrees

HUMAN

Made out of 60% water

RESOURCES

HOW YOU CAN HELP

Atticus might find it hard to spot a tiger because there are so few of them left in the wild. But with plenty of help from people who care, tiger numbers have gone from an all-time low of about 3200 in 2010 to about 5500 in 2023.
You can help by donating, volunteering or getting involved in other ways.
Here are a few organizations who can assist:

- The Global Tiger Forum (www.globaltigerforum.org)

- The International Union for Conservation of Nature
(www.iucnsos.org/initiative/integrated-tiger-habitat-conservation-programme/)

- The Wildlife Conservation Society (www.wcs.org/our-work/species/tigers)

- World Wildlife Fund (www.worldwildlife.org)

SELECTED SOURCES

◦ Britannica Online: www.britannica.com/animal/tiger

◦ International Environment Library Consortium – Tiger Fact Sheet: https://ielc.libguides.com/sdzg/factsheets/tiger

◦ International Union for Conservation of Nature Red List: www.iucnredlist.org/species/15955/214862019

◦ National Geographic Kids: www.kids.nationalgeographic.com/animals/mammals/facts/tiger

◦ Panthera: www.panthera.org/cat/tiger

• San Diego Zoo Wildlife Alliance: https://animals.sandiegozoo.org/animals/tiger

• Smithsonian's National Zoo & Conservation Biology Institute: www.nationalzoo.si.edu/animals/tiger

• World Wildlife Fund: www.worldwildlife.org/species/tiger